Uterotopia

ALSO BY RACHEL GALVIN

POETRY

Elevated Threat Level (Green Lantern Press, 2018)

Pulleys & Locomotion (Black Lawrence Press, 2009)

POETRY IN TRANSLATION

Alejandro Albarrán, *Cowboy* (Ugly Duckling Presse, 2019)

Oliverio Girondo, *Decals: Complete Early Poems*
(Open Letter Books, 2018), with Harris Feinsod

Raymond Queneau, *Hitting the Streets* (Carcanet Press, 2013)

CRITICISM

News of War: Civilian Poetry 1936–1945
(Oxford University Press, 2018)

Auden at Work (Palgrave, 2014), co-edited with Bonnie Costello

Uterotopia

Poems

Rachel Galvin

A Karen & Michael Braziller Book
PERSEA BOOKS / NEW YORK

Persea Books, Inc.
90 Broad Street
New York, New York 10004

Library of Congress Cataloging-in-Publication Data

Names: Galvin, Rachel Judith, author.
Title: Uterotopia : poems / Rachel Galvin.
Description: First. | New York : A Karen & Michale Braziller Book/Persea Books, [2022] | Summary: "Uterotopia considers sexism and aging, fertility and mortality, the bystander effect, and violence against women on an intimate and national level"—Provided by publisher.
Identifiers: LCCN 2022030797 | ISBN 9780892555659 (paperback)
Subjects: LCGFT: Poetry.
Classification: LCC PS3607.A42588 U87 2022 | DDC 811/.6--dc23/eng/20220702
LC record available at https://lccn.loc.gov/2022030797

Book design and composition by Rita Lascaro
Typeset in Sabon
Manufactured in the United States of America. Printed on acid-free paper.

Acknowledgments

Grateful thanks to the editors of the publications in which some of these poems appeared:

The Bennington Review, "Meat and Honey" and "One Sugar or Two"

Critical Quarterly, "Information Overload"

Fence, "Red Armor"

Harvard Review, "Fine Arts"

Indiana Review, "Corpse Pose"

Mississippi Review, "Corpse Pose (II)"

The Nation, "Little Death"

Ploughshares, "Kaddish for an Unborn Child"

Plume, "Why Does the Light"

The Spectacle, "Well No One Ever Said Breeding Was Easy"

"Little Death" was reprinted in *Best American Poetry 2020*, edited by David Lehman and Paisley Rekdal (Scribner, 2020).

Heartfelt gratitude to Vera Iliatova for permission to feature "Person You Choose" (2013) on the cover of this book. Her stunning paintings, which have awed me for decades, haunt my imagination and inspire several of these poems. Thank you for your brilliant art and your friendship, Vera.

Warm thanks to Gabe Fried for his editorial vision and his enthusiasm for giving this book a home at Persea Books. Thank you to everyone at Persea who helped bring this book into the world and especially to Dinah Fried for her cover design.

"Meat and Honey" was written while thinking about a Damien Hirst installation.

"Resistance" was written in conversation with the work of Anselm Kiefer.

Infinite gratitude to Ilya Kaminsky, G.C. Waldrep, and Daniel Borzutzky for endless conversation about poems and for helping make this book better. So much love and thanks to Camille Bloomfield, Alicia Mireles Christoff, Caroline Kim Brown, Miki Marin, Tina Pamintuan, Sonya Posmentier, Rachel Price, Sonali Thakkar, and Caroline Vuillemin, for, "Other women are her main source of information about what to do." All love to the Galvin clan (Sadie, Hannah, Noah, Eliza, Katie, Danny, Irene, and Tom), the memories of Joe and Libby Flum and Isabelle Gordon, and to Will Schroeder. And to Daniel, Lorenzo, and Felix, de todo corazón.

Contents

*

Uterotopia

Little Death

after Jonathas de Andrade

When a man traps a fish
he removes the hook from its side
and once it has beaten its fright
into the wooden boat with its slaps
he will clutch the fish to his chest
and hold it as it struggles
he will hold it in the tender air
He will hold its tail
as if it were his dance partner's waist
and gaze into the fish's face for minutes

When a man seizes a fish, he soothes it
caresses its body tip to tip
while it thrashes bloody against his bare chest
He will clasp the fish with one hand
like a newborn
and hush its gasping with the other
With love he will tuck it under his chin
so he can feel its heartbeat
in the insistent heat that hangs above the water

Remember: when a man captures a fish
he will seduce it while he slaughters it
the strength of his love can't be simulated
the sound of the green water can't be simulated
he will kiss the wheezing gills
his kisses can't be simulated
He will hold it as it struggles
that little death
he will hold it in the tender air

Meat and Honey

Heavy rubber curtains the doorway of a human-sized butterfly terrarium
We're instructed to proceed at a steady pace

amidst insects gorging on honey. If the creatures
had been house flies, they would have been hideous

reminding me of my own corpse rotting
None of the rainbow covenant

that's bundled into the butterfly. What if they were small foxes?
Cats? Maybe their life span is too long, but it would make

a hell of a durational piece. It's impossible to think of how many lives
are happening amidst the wriggling filaments, the legs with a single claw

impossible to think of those that have happened and ended, who are hungry
who are not at home, who are broken, who are falling right now

When I first discovered orgasms, I walked through the world in a haze
wondering why that wasn't what everyone does all day long

how can anyone talk of anything else? Now, I think the same of death
How can anyone think of anything else. I'm terribly attached

to my own consciousness, I'm at home in the scaffolding
of my mind, the taste of my knees

the smell of my armpits, the beats my feet keep and those they don't
my compound eye, my proboscis. I imagine losing this

Imagine someone else passing through the rubber curtains
watching me feed on sugar water, spin a silk mat

shrug off my exoskeleton, eat it like an edible overcoat
and fall to the floor behind a trailing plant

It's devastating and the crimson, orange, and yellow
the inexplicable gold chrysalis, make a difference—little angels

little widgets. Pumping fluid into crumpled wings
until they stiffen. Photographs are forbidden

but they'd be useless anyway, the point is to move and sweat
losing our signatures, like a dancer's unmistakable ankle

or how she lifts a shoulder with curiosity as one might lift
an eyebrow. My body inclines toward another, I sip the air

with my tubular sucking organ, I am a question
made of meat and honey

Red Armor

A man crafts the smallest sushi in the world
from one grain of rice
a tiny piece of nori
wrapped around a shred of sea urchin

He says a woman cried for over an hour
when she saw the small sushi, it was just so cute

The ratio indicating the relation of the duration
of weeping to the size of the sushi
is bewildering

Sometimes I can't tell if my neighbor upstairs is crying
As I listen to her outpouring I try to discern
whether it's giddy giggling or lament

I change my mind every few minutes
Her state of excitement is perhaps both
She must wonder this about me too sometimes

Should you punch a Nazi yes or no

Should you punch a girl sitting at a bar yes or no

If you are the girl sitting at the bar will you laugh when you tell the story
about how a guy you didn't even know walked up and punched you

I turn over my lipstick and look at the label
all this time I'd been reading "red amour" as "red armor"
I suppose that more than amour I needed armor on my mouth

If you are the girl sitting on the bar should you punch the guy back

In the 1960s the Viet Cong guerilla girls who came to visit Chile
looked like angels says the artist whose glasses read VERDAD
Some were snipers or officers, some were spies

Around here, you can't make a sound without someone seeing it

Corpse Pose

The smell of it. The smell of it

The thick pudding air

The waiting for death of it

The talking to the air of it

The one-eye blind of it. The calling you Barbara of it

The fake flower behind Beverly's ear that changes each day

Red or blue behind Beverly's ear

The smell of it. The missing legs of it

The thick smell of the air

The woman who's lost in the hallway

and wants to dance with you

The man who says you're beautiful you're all beautiful

Kind Pauline who winks

The sliding to one side and not getting back up

The sleeping mid-sentence. The smell of it

The soft skin and the knotted-up back

The dappled hands, the dappled cheeks, the soft skin

The tough nurses, the toughstrong nurses

The woman who says you're going the wrong way

and how can I get some food around here Dave

The waiting for the food on a Styrofoam plate

The half portion. The feeding like a baby is fed

The airplane spoon. The foam padding on the silverware

The curtain pulled mostly closed

The thick thick smell of it

The sign that says caution when opening door

a resident may be standing behind it

The fortified water that looks like Kool-Aid

The man who sits by the elevator

and greets women in Italian waving Ciao, ciao

The laughter of Beverly

at a story about people she's never met

The spit collecting in the corners of the mouth

The relishing of ice cream by Mrs. Isabelle P. Gordon

eating slowly in the late afternoon sun

on an unseasonably cool summer day

while wearing a blue track suit and charm necklace

The looking at the table while waiting

The humming while waiting

Dave humming while waiting

watching the greenery out the window

by the highway over the construction site

The not humming

The emergency sign

with a man running down the stairs

chased by giant flames

The thick thick smell

State of Affairs

These are my lips:
skirts draping in mud

These are my intestines:
coexisting
as I don't know how
with the bodies
of the dead

Teach me, body
the collusion
the folding down
of self

The wet clay scent of decay
says let yourself
be an instrument
of your own
recounting

Petals on the ground:
typed letters dropped
from my agitated fingers

The poem is a hormone.

Lisa Robertson, "The Seam"

Uterotopia

You want to know what's in my womb?
I'll tell you what's in my womb. A proleptic silence

my niece's shoe, graffiti, wheel of cheese
Pez dispenser, carburetor

twin cockroach corpses
overstuffed couch cushion

the key he broke in my lock, earwax
ticket stub for a half-seen film

homemade clown's nose
extra-virgin olive oil, a grimace, a toothache

the difference between live leaves and dead printer paper
that sore spot on the side of your tongue

a clock tower, cherry trees not yet
in bloom, a tangle of hangers, a duct-taped

suitcase handle, unfolded laundry
a sonogram, an echo, a question that gagged me

a spray of bamboo, a spray of unopened bills
the word *abanico*, a street in the Jewish quarter

the stained pillows in your ex-girlfriend's
ex-boyfriend's apartment

a mountain we hiked
where you couldn't say I love you

just one more time
a window where you crouched

when someone ran by shooting
through your backyard

my hiking boots tied so tightly they left
bleeding welts that healed into scars

which the Frenchmen took for bondage marks
your steel-toed boots, your helmeted noggin

your milk frother, his milk frother
my milk frother, all the frothy milk frothers

the residue the vestige the residual the verging
the incipient the impeded the thwarted the stymied

the step-laddered the step-parented the stepped-upon
the stepped-up the stopped-up the unstoppered

the unstoppable the just stop it
Husks casks coffins caskets baskets crows

cracking, crushing shells, rinds
husked skins, shucked shins, shucked nuns

nunchucks, chipmunks, monks with chips
Jesuits eating French fries

musical chairs, misbegotten messages
two girls watching from a dark window

while we kissed, drunk
who was kissing, who was watching

who was screwing while who was being screwed
who tried to place a hand upon those who were screwing

but was gently nudged away
who grabbed whose pointy tit

which pup was shushed, which venetian blind
flipped up, panting pup

the yipping pup doesn't know what's up
waxing moon, gibbous moon, bikini waxing

winding up your winnings, wishing
the whorled tongue would, would world

would footsteps, would stop feet, would step upon
step up, set up, set down, set upon, set out, set forth

set forth, set forth, set forth, set forth, follow through

Corpse Pose

Pretend you are dead and we will eat you
my four-year-old nieces insist I lie still
and close my eyes

Pretend that you're REALLY dead
They make munching sounds (*yum yum*)
while pretending to eat my torso

Then S grabs her doll, saying
I'm going to eat this baby, yum yum

At night I look into the mirror and whisper
Hello baby
pretend you are dead and begin chewing

*

At the Hyowon Healing Center in South Korea
you can practice your own death

in the company of others
write your own obituary
and give it a trial run

among candles and chrysanthemums
you may say prayers
put on a yellow or white burial shroud
and the Envoy from the Other World
will nail you into a casket for ten dark minutes
You may photograph yourself with your coffin

*

When M's parents brought him for a grave viewing
in Rockaway Beach
so he could admire their fine vista
and see his own grave with a view
he waited til his parents had just faded from view
then pissed on his grave with gusto

*

An eight-hundred-year-old churchyard
reclines under the rotting apples in Oliver's orchard
Toddlers grab green yellow red apples with glee
a wanton bite here, toss it away, a bite there, toss it away
Child becomes apple becomes child

The young doctor jokes
*We're going to put you in the juicing machine,
we'll make Fred juice, how about that, we'll drink you up!*

To which five-year-old Fred replies
I'm not an apple!
But we all know he is

*

The Met was evacuated
when Roger threw ashes
white as anthrax
into the orchestra pit
ashes he later said

were the remains of a friend
whom he wanted to scatter
within the houses of music

so he could listen forever
a tender dismemberment
as remembrance
with the Met as ninth stop
on his opera tour

Trying to lighten the mood
I told Terry
they would never be able to vacuum
all of him up

*

Twice today I've seen squirrel carcasses
mashed into the ground by cars
Fur like small flags, grave markers

*

It is the eleventh year of the war
against the drug cartels
At least 150,000 people have died

A girl paints a second mouth
made of marigolds
on the side of her face

Decapitated, disappeared, buried
in clandestine graves, thrown in garbage dumps

Only chins and hair visible
women wearing skeleton masks
march in remembrance of the six women
killed every day near Juárez

reduced to ashes, drowned in sewage canals

The lady who cuts the umbilical cord
watches over their bones

*

My four-year-old nieces are playing with a doll they call Aunt Sofia
Aunt Sofia falls off the third-story balcony and says *ouch*

She is taken to the hospital and receives new legs
new arms and a new head

Aunt Sofia falls off the balcony again
and falls off the balcony and falls off

Aunt Sofia falls off the balcony again
and the lady who cuts the umbilical cord
watches over her bones

One Sugar or Two

In Chicago urban farmers have such a surplus of eggs
they don't even barter
they just give them away

On the table is served a Dutch baby
made of 6 eggs, 8 tablespoons of butter
a little flour, a little milk, a pinch of nutmeg
a Dutch baby
right out of the oven
Give me a piece of that baby, she says
Put some hot sauce on that baby, he says

I'm reminded of a man in Vermont pulling a stillborn sheep
out from its moaning mother

The one born alive has cords wrapped around it
spindly legs that seem impossible
but within a week
the lamb is playing king of the mountain
atop a heap of dung

Sheepskin on the sofa, sheepskin on the floor

I think of my friend's poem about the futility
of writing poems about birthing animals
about pulling anything from death into life

Kids before guns, the teenager yells into the mike
to a crowd of half a million at the Capitol

A gun without bullets is sold out of a truck for 200 bucks
to pay for dinner
With bullets, you can afford dessert

We don't actually need assault weapons to kill deer
a child hunter comments

This morning high school students across the country
walked out to protest gun violence

while at the same moment
a man walked into a Florida high school
and shot a student

In Florida almost all manatees bear scars from boat propellers
one is nicknamed No Tail
everyone is especially sad when a boat kills a manatee
that has what they call a milk-dependent baby

Local Produce, Or, Womb Yam Dithyramb

C goes to the gynecologist
to investigate a gnawing
in her abdomen
A tuberous grumbling
when she walks
For several weeks
spongey protuberances grow
roots with fine hair like cilia
long enough to tug at
Bright green lobed leaves
she doesn't dare trim back
This is a true story

C's gynecologist dons goggles
inserts a speculum, explaining
C is growing sweet tasting
ipomoea batatas, a sweet potato
or rather several

which is to say C has cultivated
yams in her womb
high in B vitamins
at a pH range of 4.5 to 7.0
Mature in 2 to 9 months
and from the looks of it
ripe and ready to stir fry

Does she want the crop harvested?
C nods and her gynecologist culls the tubers
places them in a jar
by other root vegetable specimens
an organic market cultivated

if not by hand, by womb.
A womb salad. A female farrago

Is this a true story
an urban pastoral, or a lullaby?

Sleep now, the ladies are growing legumes
sleep now, the time for babies
has passed, the ladies are busy germinating
Sleep, they are sprouting your supper

Hostile Uterus

What do I carry? A glowing orb, an orbit
an orifice, this uterus, this bright bulb

yes that's right, it's a uterus lightbulb
it sits on my hips like a lid

on a ceramic sugar bowl marked CYANIDE
it is texting madly while waiting at a bus stop

watching the wind pick up and the hail begin
it is hailing the bus driver, it is driving the bus

my uterus lightbulb is driving the bus

❧

Darás tu obra como se da un hijo:
restando sangre de tu corazón.

You will birth your work as one births a child:
by subtracting blood from your heart.

Gabriela Mistral, "Decálogo del artista"

Well No One Ever Said Breeding Was Easy

(Braided Abecedarian)

Attempts for years to have a child
gives up, adopts a child, gets pregnant

> Zipping your lips is what they call it
> when you pretend it doesn't hurt

Budgets for four rounds of IVF
has three miscarriages, one healthy baby

> You should just adopt, people say

Ceases taking depression meds
so as to conceive and grows suicidal

> X-rays are what they call it when they squirt you full
> of iodine to check your tubes

Delivers a stillborn baby, then miscarries

> Wage gap is what they call it when women make 77 cents
> for every dollar earned by men

Eclampsia is what they call the seizures
that land her in the hospital in her eighth month

> Visa officers block pregnant women at the border
> for fear of what they call anchor babies

Freezes six embryos just in case
then gets pregnant by accident

Uterine cancer is what they call it
when you're exposed to toxic chemical waste

Geriatric mother is what the doctors call you
when you're pregnant over 35

Transvaginal probes are what they put inside you
when you seek an abortion in 27 states

Has an abortion, has an abortion, has a miscarriage

Senile vaginitis is what the doctors call it
when you're in menopause

I lost at least one book, maybe one and a half
to raising my kids, she says

Runs a marathon while bleeding freely
blood staining her leggings

Just home from the hospital with her newborn
when her wife leaves her

Quits her job, drops off each kid
with a different relative, and drives away

Keeps trying, keeps trying, keeps trying, keeps trying
keeps trying, keeps trying, keeps trying

Pregnancy wastage is what they write on her chart
meaning her baby is stillborn

Laughs out loud when she discovers she's pregnant at fifty

Other women are her main source of information
about what to do

Married for fifteen years and can't convince her husband
to have a child

Not expecting her period, she wads up toilet paper
in her panties but still bleeds through

Never wanted to have kids and is now stepmother to three

Mother makes her sleep in the cow shed until her period is over

Ovaries are hyperstimulated by IVF drugs
and she gains 15 pounds in one week

Luxury items are how tampons and pads are classified
for taxation in 33 states

Pretends everything is just swell
as she miscarries during a job interview

Keeps quiet when people call him the mother
even though he birthed their baby after transitioning

Questions her choice to have a child
to strangers in bars for years

Jails and prisons in the U.S. force women to work 21 hours
for a box of pads, 27 hours for a box of tampons

Resolves to have a baby on her own
and meets a new partner while seven months pregnant

Incompetent cervix or inadequate pelvis
is what they like to say to lay the blame on you

Suffers the loss of one twin in utero
and the second stays in intensive care for a year

Hostile uterus is what they call it
when your body blocks sperm like a champ

Tells no one she is pregnant, not even her partner
until the abortion is over

Good news, it hurts like hell, but I swear
you won't even remember it later

Used a donor egg and smiles every time someone says her son looks like her

Fair practice is what they call it when she doesn't get promoted
because they suspect she might have another child

Vacuuming the eggs out of her ovaries leaves her aching when she wakes

Exhausted by people mistaking her for the nanny
because she and her son don't have the same skin color

Why don't you just adopt? people ask

Decides to give up her newborn for adoption
because she wants to finish high school

X-rays of her fallopian tubes hurt more than expected
returning to work after the procedure

C-sections mean the doctor gets paid more
and they're in and out in an hour

You should think about just adopting
people advise

Buys food but no tampons this month
because she is too broke

Zygotes are overrated
says her friend with no kids

Adoption isn't an option, she can't opt to adopt
because she's broke, too broke, she's broke

Why Does the Light

The newspaper publishes a photograph of the room
where a sixteen-year-old girl
was raped by a man before onlookers
as the village council ordered
The newspaper says this happened in vengeance
for the rape of the man's twelve-year-old sister
Why does the photograph show two beds
Why do the beds have red knobs on them
Why does the photograph show a metal fan standing at center
Why does the photograph show four latched coffin-sized
metal trunks. Why is the floor dirty
Why does the photograph show a flowered scarf and a pillow
Why does the photograph show a pitcher and a covered pot
The newspaper says the girl's mother filed a complaint
The newspaper says this incident resembles other incidents
Why does the light enter through a window

Information Overload

She looks almost casual
she's collateral
it will never be clear if the girl who found her
actually saw her
never clear if the other two girls saw her
and walked on by

Here's the point of realism (*Get away from me*)
the place where the sash that binds the world is softest
and most willing to be touched
the place that smells of honeysuckle
this is the moment before

When a woman falls on the sidewalk
and yelps and yelps
the crowd pulls back

Get away from me I don't know you

When a woman entering the El
balks at the turnstile, clutches her stomach
crying out words no one understands
the crowd pulls back

What's going on?

When a woman falls to her knees
on a bridge over the river
the crowd keeps on crossing

Do I know you
Are we strangers

Does this require immediate action
Do you deserve my help

I'm not cold-hearted
but you see
I'm experiencing information overload
I'm sure you're familiar with the symptoms

Get away from me I don't know you

Did you help or hurt or did you both help and hurt
Did he attack you in my neighborhood
Did he attack you on my street
Do you look like me
Do you speak my language
Are you wearing my team's jersey
Who covered it up
Was he a priest
Will I lose my job

Get away from me I don't know you

Are you embarrassed
Are you competitive
Do you make a joke
Is she really a friend
Are you calculating your risk

It's not your problem
Would you be charged for the medical bills
Maybe you're feeling tired and apathetic
Maybe you don't want to stand out

Will you line up to watch the suicide the hanging
the lynching

What if she's your cousin
She's in her pajamas lying on the curb
her belongings in plastic bags
a taxi driver parks next to her

What if it's your ex-husband
and she starts to scream

Often this is not a parable
and this is often

A woman scavenging rubbish picks up
a two-year-old girl
after she's been hit by a van and then a truck

Will you vault the balcony
scale five stories to grab the dangling child
Will you jump into the icy water

Will you hit the attacker with a lead pipe
Will you hit the attacker with a skateboard

Often this is not a parable
and this is often

I don't mean any harm, I mean to help
I'm already singing the low song

There's no one else around
though I am scanning for them

Tender Commodities

People migrate by crowded bus or by crowded car
People cling to a freight train or an inflatable raft
No blankets, no diapers, no pads, no formula, no food

People travel by foot and travel by night and they wait
A boy falls off a freight car and breaks both arms
People wait in encampments for their children and they wait

Caged children's bodies are wrapped in Mylar
like tender commodities like bags of chips like hand grenades
They wait for frozen cheese sandwiches as snow falls like ash

They wait all day to play in a fenced-in courtyard
while around the block the restaurants keep filling
with people and emptying and filling and I think

about the work it takes to prepare those meals
and serve them: crops grown, produce picked, food shipped
linens bleached, tables bused, credit cards charged

A weary swirl of finance crowds around the waste
So many items so many items so very many items and items
I think about who's making who's buying who's using all the items

Tender commodities like the bodies of detained children
Children sleep in a retail store cuddled by ghost commodities
nestled in rows upon rows of chain-link fence, fluorescent lights

all day all night agents and cameras and agents and cameras
bed pads on the concrete and bed pads on the concrete and wet wipes
and wet wipes and wet wipes instead of showers and bags of chips
and bags of chips and bags of chips and bags of chips

∗✦∗

Occasionally you pull out a dead rabbit from your panties.
Every month you pull out a dead rabbit and hang it on the wall.
On the wall you hang a crying that smells like rabbits' ears.

Kim Hyesoon, "Calendar: Day Two,"
translated by Don Mee Choi

Fine Arts

after W.H. Auden

About women she is never wrong
the young painter: how well she understands
their predicament: how they must resemble bright red poppies

while someone else watches them eat or take off their coat or just walk
    down the street

How, when the old men are passionately waiting
for them to bend and reveal their cleavage, there must always be
girls who are still children, who did not at all want it to happen, strolling
by a pond at the edge of the wood:
she never forgets
that it keeps on happening
anyway in a corner, some humdrum place
where men get on with their lives and their locker room pranks
scratching their balls and the ears of devoted dogs

In Vera Iliatova's *Softly, Softly,* for instance:
how two girls grab hands and turn away
when they see the body lying in blood; a third in a blue scarf may
have heard the screaming or heard the silence after
but she did not know what to do; the sun went on shining
as it had to on the girls disappearing into the grass
disappearing into the river, disappearing into the desert
and the indigo blur of a neck elegantly turned away
belonged to someone who might have seen something
but had things to do and went on with their day

Uterotopiary

Or, Excuse Me, You Have a Garden on Your Face

Sixteenth-century Frenchmen
collected anatomical blazons
in an anthology celebrating and preserving
accounts of women's extraordinary parts

Each term of comparison
was also an assertion
that the man possessed her
and possessed other options
This was part of his power
The pertinent point
was his ability to wound a woman

To blazon, as in, to represent
to describe in detail
to display to proclaim
to broadcast

That must be a pretty picture
you dropping to your knees
says the presidential candidate
to a female contestant on TV

The other pertinent point
was his power to wound a woman
by displaying his familiarity
with the feel of her breasts and so on

Thus he named the ladies
and their parts
so that the words
comprised a dummy
of his absent beloved

What happened
to the powerful women
of South America?
inquires *The New York Times*
Is gender a factor?

The collective decline
of three women leaders
points to a persistence
of masculinist attitudes
in the region
especially within
the political establishment

It's as if women leaders
are getting all the backlash
for the corruption of men
says Dr. Farida Jalalzai

A gargantuan woman
reclines in topiary
the curve of her lips
leads to the curve of her hips
crowds marvel at the living statue
The gardener
has trimmed her just so

Did you know modern feminism
is all about grooming?
blogs a blogger

Let's irrigate the topiaries

If women farmers had the same resources as men
the number of hungry people in the world
would be reduced by 150 million
says a press release
titled Women hold the key to building a world
free from hunger and poverty

Half of agricultural laborers are women
yet they own less than 20 percent of land

Among hungry people
60 percent are women or girls

They call it a gap a gender gap
These are facts
Hunger is a fact

Let's irrigate the topiaries

Irrigate the topiaries

Irrigate the topiaries

Let's irrigate

Ovaries Over Easy

My uterus is a cinema cigarette girl
standing with arms akimbo
fists balled on each hip

A tray of bonbons and chicles
balances across her chest
on a velvet cord

She wears leather pants
and answers the front door
saying *Drink?*

My uterus is an opera singer
opening her arms
to cloak her listeners in song

She resembles a flying fox
her forelimbs are webbed wings
she flaps her fingers to fly

She emerges at twilight
hunts by echolocation

She clasps her follicles
like un-flung Frisbees

When she strolls along Lake Michigan
she balances her ovaries
like two dessert goblets of raspberry Jell-O

Each hipbone
offers a real-fruit confection
to the lake's diminutive unsalted waves
one at a time, hello, hello

My ovaries snap like castanets
My uterus juggles her tumblers
proffers her pockets as petri dishes

She tweaks her own nipples
She is her own tightrope

Balancing on one foot
she is a minyan of women

Empty Rooms

One girl is more plural
one is at least eleven selves
one is pressed into the background

like a skull left unburied
or a thumbprint in excrement

I walk ahead of my alternate selves
those I left in another country
with the children I will not bear

Do I expend the women I once was
as I walk?

Some days I feel them
hovering by my head like dybbuks

Unclear if I am diving
into lambent memory
or just diving in

heaving with thirst
I drink at a rusty fountain

Did you say benevolent or malevolent?
They sound so similar

I'm standing in the shadows of the forest
watching my self-persuasion sprout

Faces I cancel
faces I delete

She and her and her and she
My attention flickers

Menstruation is omnivorous

No one owes me anything

Unclear if I'm diving into flames that I kindled
or if someone else set the fire
but I don't really need to know, nor do you

I must decide how many women to become
it's hard to decide in advance

at each opening of the skin, a tally
each bleeding counted

The weight of all the things I don't say
makes me sleepy

My womb glistens
with a subpar diamond shard
they call a bort

That woman in the forest may be watching her footing
or her footage but I swear I see her half-smile

as she walks this very stretch of road
yes and yellow and yes and yellow

I can make out a breast a sternum
a buttock some limbs

but when I shut my eyes
my retinas produce electrical charges
that blaze and buzz, dividing like cells

Still, by the fire blossom
Still, by the smear of fire, still, embryonic flame

It would be easy, it would all be easier
if everyone would just do what I wanted:
blood or flames or both

You Can Always Freeze Your Eggs

A Ballad

I can't face my body when the evening
is over and one by one everyone grows
with their families toward evening and evening
and alone to my apartment I go

It's me and the buzz of the fridge, the fridge
is me, my opera, my anthem, my buzz, my ballad
My body, she drifts over the bridge
while I worry about the planted

irises gone rotten, were they a prophecy?
I worry my fuzzy eggs are stacked
in my ovaries' hapless pockets
like the cartons of mush I scrapped

since I forgot all March and April
as they squatted in the dark fridge
Today I break each month in the pail
one at a time, smashing each shell on the ridge

smashing them because I didn't know
smashing the months because I forgot, because I can't
forget, smashing because I didn't hear the bells or feel the toll
and I have to break them to see them run

In the Seam of Life

In the mirror I'm watching my alternate life
I mean: this life I seem to be living is actually the other life I might have lived

You know how you or your friends sometimes think
what if I hadn't married X or taken that job or had those kids?

Oh I should've been a pianist, my high school social studies teacher
used to tell me. Oh I should've been an actor, my father would say

I always wonder what kind of sex life
I would have if I didn't have those two boys, my friend confides

over a glass of wine. Maybe I would be sleeping with women
instead of men. Yes, definitely sleeping with women

Here I am dancing before a mirror watching my alternate life unfold
I've kept my figure, as they say. I have a night life and a sex life

and a creative life and an intellectual life and I'm even growing
some plant life on my windowsill and some bacterial life in my shower

Watching myself dance in the middle of these years
in which I am single and living alone. What am I getting at?

What I'm trying to describe to you isn't déjà vu
it's more like the rumble of a movie playing in the theater next door

Families eating laughing arguing putting food on each other's plates
as I trudge through the snow by a fleet of restaurants docked liked cruise ships

I switch to a film in which I too have a family and am putting some food
on my daughter's plate, I greet my other life in an effusion of glowing lights

I note how the feeling of comfort and assured futurity is made manifest
by a mass-produced lamp that glows Relaxing Golden Amber #60

The truth is I long for the lamps the messy plates the children's laughter
but I don't know how to enter the restaurant I'm passing by

on a frozen April evening. It used to bother me more, but now
I see that even if there were one, I couldn't find the door

❧

We are difficult, God
We're going to nurse the hell out of whatever you serve us

Resistance

the graveyards were bombed,
and the immortal dead,
of vigilant bones and everlasting shoulder, on their graves,
the immortal dead, on feeling, seeing, hearing,
so low the evil, so dead the vile aggressors,
resumed their unfinished mourning

César Vallejo, trans. Valentino Gianuzzi and Michael Smith

On the bed, a stain in the shape of a state
or a city, no, it's shaped like a small town

that belongs to one country
invaded by another country

now reclaimed by the first country
though the inhabitants never hold citizenship

in any sovereign nation
their town batted back and forth

two dogs killing a mouse

remember the bombed graveyard next door
headstones in shards

even the dead are not safe the dead are not safe
they are not safe, they are not, not the dead

the bed sits in a room filled with guilt vinegar
rust and shame, vinegar frustration

dead stalks, greyed-out honeycombed heads
women made of wire

a militarized border striates the room
grave markers drape over the lead bed

even the dead are not safe, the dead are not safe
they are not safe, they are not, not the dead

the women who sleep in the bed build boats of rust
to sail on a sea of rust amidst scum and froth

mud and lead, breathing camphor
breathing vinegar, breathing the burnt

smudges where water used to be, ash
still ash, dirt encrusted in cracks

ash, boats built of rust to sail on a sea of rust
ash, words scratched in flesh, words etched

where sky had been, ash
boats laden with refuse, boats of scrap

a horizon scratched into the sky's husk, ash
waves etched in rust, ash on wire, ash on rust

water-stained scraps jut through waves of wire
waves of ash, the sea burnt and cracked

the sea needs camphor, the sea needs ash
rub camphor on the sea

its lacerations and sores, the sea is sore
so sore, the sea is sore, rust is growing

encroaching, rub camphor on the sea
blisters of the sea

let boats of ash sail on the sea of blisters
let the boats scrape across the sea of wire

sea of rust, sea of ash
let the boats scratch waves of wire

waves of ash
let the boats scrape and scratch

for even the dead are not safe, the dead are not safe
they are not safe, they are not, not the dead

Kaddish for an Unborn Child

So that you feel the weight of your life, you
and the children you do not have
you and the children, you
and you and the children and you

So that your days may be lengthened
and tightened by children
so that the days of your life may be darkened
and so that you may be decreased
all the days of your life

These words, bone shards in your heart muscle
you try to teach the children
the words you do not have
you teach them words
and how to speak of children you do not have

when you sit alone in your house
with no words
when you walk alone along your way
without children
when you lie down alone
and when alone you rise

You bind them as a sign
each syllable upon your hand
that raises no children
from any consonant

they glint like mirrors
the silences between your eyes
that open to see no children

You inscribe this silence
again and again
on the doorposts of your house

When you enter a nation
of thriving cities you did not build

houses full of all the good things you didn't gather
and vineyards and olive trees you didn't plant
you will eat alone and taste only salt

Your work on this earth is finite
Your name and your children will be salt

Do not seek the gods of people around you
or the salt to which you don't belong

for if you do, your death will be kindled against you
like the lights within your womb you didn't keep lit

If the daughter you do not have
comes to you in your sleep and asks you
where you have hidden her

say to her, I was given signs I didn't heed
What did I see? I saw the stone hand of death

The stone hand of what? The stone
in the hand of death but I did not fear
I've never feared enough

If the daughter you do not have
comes to you in your sleep and asks you where
you have hidden her, say to her I saw
I saw the hand of stone

Slowly I Erase Our Selves

I smear you I smudge you
I paint you
with my inky hair
trace a ghost transcript
of our conversation
on the noisy doorposts
of your body
your body, a scripture I decipher
with love
forsaken adverbs, lost nouns
unmarked vowels

my hair composes a Talmudic commentary
on your body, in columns
with footnotes in the margins
enveloping your body
with my queries my polemics
my elaborations

I wrap your body in my inky hair
in my hair-ink, my tefillin
each strand is a shouting hair-strand
the tip of my dripping hair
encircles your nipples
encircles your neck, encircles
your armpit, your pelvis

Slowly slowly with love
I smear you I smudge you
with love I dip you I drench you
I am the waters pouring over you
you glisten with my fluids
my calligraphic fluids

About the Author

RACHEL GALVIN is the author of the poetry collections *Elevated Threat Level* and *Pulleys & Locomotion*. She is the translator of Raymond Queneau's *Hitting the Streets*, which won the 2014 Scott Moncrieff Prize, and co-translator of *Decals: Complete Early Poems of Oliverio Girondo*, a finalist for the 2019 National Translation Award. Her translation of *Cowboy & Other Poems*, a chapbook by Alejandro Albarrán Polanco, appeared in 2019. She is a co-founder of Outranspo, an international creative translation collective (outranspo.com), and was a 2021–2022 National Endowment for the Arts literature translation fellow. Her work appears in journals and anthologies including *Best American Experimental Writing 2020, Best American Poetry 2020, Bennington Review, Boston Review, Colorado Review, Fence, Harvard Review, McSweeney's, The Nation, The New Yorker, Ploughshares, Plume,* and *Poetry*. She is the author of a work of criticism, *News of War: Civilian Poetry, 1936–1945,* and is an associate professor at the University of Chicago.